A *Fowl*

ALPHABET

A Fowl ALPHABET

Illustrations by Alan James Robinson

Lettering by Suzanne Moore

∎

Chronicle Books • San Francisco

Library of Congress Cataloging in Publication Data
Robinson, Alan James.
  A fowl alphabet.
    1. Robinson, Alan James. 2. Birds in art. 3. English
    language–Alphabet. I. Moore, Suzanne. II. Title.
ND1839.R58A4   1988   759.13   88-18925
ISBN 0-87701-524-4
Distributed in Canada by Raincoast Books,
112 East Third Avenue, Vancouver, B.C. V5T 1C8
10 9 8 7 6 5 4 3 2 1

Editor's note: The text for *Xenops* was written
by Alan James Robinson.

Chronicle Books
275 Fifth Street
San Francisco, California
94103

The most conspicuous external characteristic by which the BIRDS are distinguished from all other inhabitants of earth, is the feathery robe which invests their bodies, and which serves the double purpose of clothing and progression. For the first of these two objects it is admirably adapted, as the long, slender filaments of the feathers are not only in themselves indifferent conductors of heat,... and thus preserves the bird in a moderate temperature through the icy blasts of winter or the burning rays of summer sun. A similar function is discharged by the furry coats of many mammalia; but the feathers serve another office, which is not possessed by hair or fur. They aid the creature in progression, and enable it to raise and sustain itself in the atmosphere. Towards the promotion of this latter function the entire structure of the body and limbs is obviously subservient, and even in the comparatively rare instances where the bird—such as the penguin, ostrich, or the kiwi-kiwi—is destitute of flying powers, the general idea of a flying creature is still preserved.

The chief and most obvious distinctive feature in the skull of a bird and of a mammal lies in the jaw-bones, which in the bird are entirely toothless, and are covered at their extremities with a peculiar horny incrustment, termed the beak or bill. This bill is of very different shape in the various tribes of birds; being in some cases strong, sharp, and curved, as in the birds of prey; in others long, slender, and delicate, as in the creepers and humming-birds; and in others flat, spoon-like, soft, and sensitive, as in the ducks....

THE FOWL

In the arrangement of the various species of living creatures which possess a visible organization, the greater or lesser perfection of the structure has formed the basis of systematic classification. A classification of birds depends largely on the shapes of their beaks or bills. There are many other curious and interesting details of their anatomy, but this edition will consider the more bizarre and diverse examples of the beaks through bird portraiture.

■

AUK
Pinguinus impennis

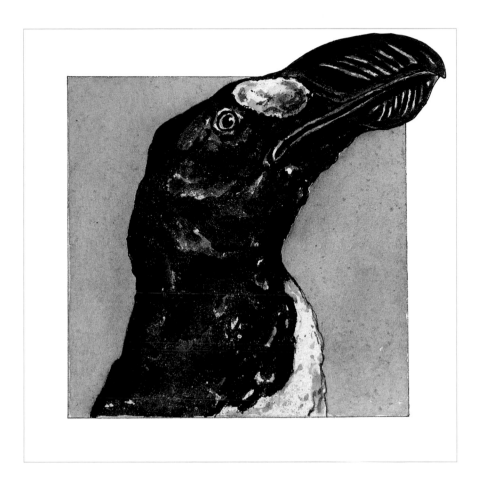

Among the several representatives of the
sub-family of the Alcinæ, or Auks, the Great *AUK* is the rarest.
This bird, formerly to be found in several parts of Northern Europe, and in
Labrador, has not been observed for many years, and is thought
to be as completely extinct as the Dodo.

BLUE-FOOTED BOOBY
Sula nebouxii

*T*he well-known *BOOBY*, so called from its
stupidity when attacked, whether by man or the frigate bird, is
closely allied to the gannet. This bird is found in most of the warmer latitudes,
settled upon the islands and rocky shores, and catching fish all day for the
benefit of the frigate birds who attack and rob it....

■

CASSOWARY
Casuarius casuarius

The well-known CASSOWARY, long
thought to be the only example of the genus, is
found in the Malaccas. This fine bird is notable for the
glossy black hair-like plumage, the helmet-like protuberance upon
the head, and the light azure, purple and scarlet of the upper part of the neck.
The "helmet" is a truly remarkable apparatus, being composed of a
honey-combed cellular bony substance, made on a principle that much
resembles the structure of the elephant's skull,... The beak is high
in proportion to its width, and is therefore unlike the flattened
and comparatively weak bills of the Ostrich.

■

DODO
Raphus cucullatus

The position held by the celebrated
DODO among birds was long doubtful, and was
only settled in comparatively late years by careful examination
of the few relics which are our sole and scanty records of this very
remarkable bird...."It has a great ill-favored head, covered with a kind of
membrane, resembling a hood; great black eyes; a bending, prominent,
fat neck; an extraordinary long, strong, bluish-white bill, only the
ends of each mandible are a different color, that of the upper
black, that of the nether yellowish, both sharp-pointed
and crooked. Its gape, huge wide, as being
naturally very voracious...."

■

EMU
Dromaius novæhollandiæ

The EMEU [sic] is not unlike the ostrich,
which it resembles in many of its habits as well as in its form
and general aspect. It is very swift of foot, but can be run down by horses
and dogs without much difficulty.

■

FLAMINGO
Phœnicopterus ruber

The well-known *FLAMINGO* brings us to
the large and important order of Anseres, of the goose
tribe....When feeding the Flamingo bends its neck, and placing the
upper mandible of the curiously-bent beak on the ground or under the water,
separates the nutritive portions with a kind of spattering sound,
like that of a duck when feeding.

◼

GOATSUCKER
Caprimulgus carolinensis

The GOAT-SUCKERS, as they are
familiarly termed, from a stupid notion that was formerly in
great vogue among farmers, and is not even yet quite extinct, that these
birds were in the habit of sucking wild goats, cows, and sheep,... The gape of the
mouth is so large that when the bird opens its beak to its fullest
extent, it seems to have been severely wounded across
the mouth,...

HORNBILL
Buceros bicornus

*T*here are many strange and
wonderful forms among the feathered tribes; but
there are, perhaps, none which more astonish the
beholder who sees them for the first time, than the group of
birds known by the name of *HORNBILLS*. They are all distinguished
by a very large beak, to which is added a singular helmet-like appendage,
equalling the beak itself in some species, while in others it is so small as to attract
but little notice. On account of the enormous size of the beak and the helmet,
which in some species recede to the crown of the head, the bird
appears to be overweighted by the mass of horny substance
which it has to carry; but on a closer investigation, the
whole structure is found to be singularly light,
and yet very strong.

■

IBIS
Eudocimus albus

Wood *IBIS*. This is a bird of considerable
size for an ibis.... It is a remarkable and interesting bird.
It resembles a crane, being nearly four feet in length; standing higher than that
when erect. It is pure white, with the tips of wings and the tail black. The adult
bird has an entirely bald head, and an enormously thick,
heavy bill, tapering and a little decurved.

JACANA
Parra spinosa

The general color of the common
JACANA is black, with a slight greenish gloss, taking a rusty
red tinting on the back and wing-coverts.... At the base of the beak is
a curious feathery appendage, rising upon the forehead above and
depending towards the chin below.

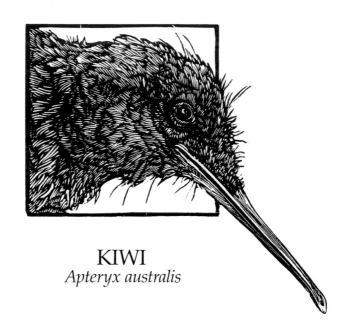

KIWI
Apteryx australis

*P*erhaps the very strangest and most
weird-like of all living birds is the Apteryx, or
KIWI-KIWI.... This singular bird is a native of New
Zealand, where it was once very common, but, like the
dinornis, is in a fair way of becoming extinct, a fate from which it has
probably been hitherto preserved by its nocturnal and retiring habits....
The long curved beak of the Apteryx has the nostrils very narrow,
very small, and set on at each side of the tip, so that the bird is
enabled to pry out the worms and other nocturnal creatures
on which it feeds, without trusting only to the eyes....

LOON
Gavia immer

The LOON is a well-known bird, yet it is
not often seen. It is large and striking in appearance, and the
plumage in the male is very beautiful.

■

MACAW
Ara macao

The MACAWS are mostly inhabitants of
Southern America, in which country so many magnificent
birds find their home.... They are all very splendid birds, and are
remarkable for their great size, their very long tails, and the splendid hues of their
plumage. The beak is also very large and powerful, and in some
species the ring round the eyes and part of the face
is devoid of covering.

NUTHATCH
Sitta carolinensis

The Nuthatches form another group of the
Certhidæ, and are represented in Europe by the common
NUTHATCH of our woods. They are all remarkable for their peculiarly
stout and sturdy build, their strong, pointed, cylindrical beaks,
and their very short tails....

■

OWL
Nyctaca scandiaca

The Snowy OWL is one of the handsomest
of this group, not so much on account of its dimensions,
which are not very considerable, but by reason of the beautiful white
mantle with which it is clothed, and the large orange eyeballs that shine
with a lustre as of a living topaz set among the snowy plumage.

PUFFIN
Fratercula arctica

The odd little *PUFFIN* is remarkable for
the singular shape, enormous size, and light colors of its beak,
which really looks as if it had been originally made for some much larger
bird. Owing to the dimensions of the beak it is often called the
Sea Parrot, or the Coulterner.

QUETZAL
Pharomachrus mocino

*O*f all the birds of the air there is hardly any
which excites so much admiration as the Resplendent Trogon
[QUETZAL]. Many, such as the humming-bird, are gifted with greater
brilliancy of color; but for gorgeousness of hue, exquisite blending of tints, elegance
of contour and flowing grace of plumage, there is no worthy
rival in all the feathered tribe.

ROADRUNNER
Geococcyz californianus

A kind of Ground Cuckoo is found
inhabiting the Southwest and Mexico. It is the Chaparral
Cock, Paisano, or *ROADRUNNER*. The latter term explains its habit
of frequenting the highways, always on the ground, where it will
outrun the fleetest horses.

SPOONBILL
Ajaia ajaja

*T*he well-known SPOONBILL
affords another instance of the endless variety of
forms assumed by the same organ under different conditions;
both the beak and the windpipe being modified in a very remarkable manner,...
this species is one of the waders, frequenting the waters, and obtaining
a subsistence from the fish, reptiles, and smaller aquatic inhabitants,
which it captures in the broad, spoon-like extremity of its beak....
The beak of an adult Spoonbill is about eight inches in length,
very much flattened, and is channelled and
grooved at the base.

∎

TOUCAN
Ramphastos sulfuratus

$\mathcal{T}$he very curious birds
that go by the name of *TOUCANS* are not one whit
less remarkable than the hornbills, their beak being often as extravagantly large,
and their colors by far superior.... The most extraordinary part of these birds
is the enormous beak, which in some species,... is of gigantic dimensions,
seeming big enough to give its owner a perpetual headache,...
As in the case of the hornbills, their beak is very thin and
is strengthened by a vast number of honeycomb-cells,
so that it is very light and does not incommode
the bird in the least.

■

UMBRELLA BIRD
Cephalopterus ornatus

The UMBRELLA BIRD,... is a truly
remarkable creature, and from the extraordinary
mode in which its plumage is arranged, never fails of attracting
the attention of the most casual spectator.... In dimensions the Umbrella Bird
equals the common Carrion Crow, and but for the curious plume
which adorns its head, and the tuft which hangs from its breast,
might be mistaken at a distance for that bird.

VULTURE
Cathartes aura

All the birds of prey, called scientifically
Raptatores, or Accipitres, are readily known by their
compressed and hooked beaks. The *VULTURES* are distinguished
by the shape of the beak, which is of moderate size, nearly straight above,
curved suddenly and rounded at the tip, and without any "teeth" in the upper
mandible. In the greater number of species the head and upper part
of the neck are nearly naked, and the eyes are unshaded by the
feathery ridge which overhangs these organs in the eagles.

WHALEHEAD
Balæniceps rex

The singular *WHALE-HEADED STORK*
is the most striking of its tribe.... The chief point in this
fine bird is the huge bill, which from its resemblance in size
and shape to a shoe, has gained its owner a second title, namely,
Shoe-bird. It is enormously expanded at each side of the beak, the edges
of the upper mandible overhang those of the lower, and its tip is
furnished with a large hook, curved and sharp as that of
an eagle, and well suited for tearing to pieces the
substances on which the bird feeds.

XENOPS
Xenops minitus

The Plain *XENOPS*, a handsome
inhabitant of Mexico and Southern America, is readily
identified by its white cheek patch and the long, pale patch over and
behind its eye. Its stout, upturned bill of pale horn is ideal for hollowing out nest
cavities and for extracting insects and their larvae by
hammering at decayed vegetation.

■

YELPER [AVOCET]
Recurvirostra americana

he Avocet *[YELPER]* is one of the most
remarkable among birds, and is easily recognizable by its long,
curiously-curved beak, and its boldly pied plumage.

■

ZIGZAG HERON
Zebrilus undulatus

The long beak of the [ZIGZAG] HERON
is very sharp and dagger-like, and can be used with terrible
force as an offensive weapon. The bird instinctively aims its blow
at the eye of its adversary, and if incautiously handled is sure to deliver
a stroke quick as lightning at the captor's eye. The beak of
a species of Heron set up on a stick is used by some
savage tribes as a spear.

The text is from
ANIMATE CREATION
popular edition of OUR LIVING WORLD, A Natural History
by Rev. J.G. Wood, Vol. II, BIRDS, 1885.